W9-ANP-626

Exploring Infrastructure

PORTS

Kevin Reilly

Enslow Publishing
101 W. 23rd Street
Suite 240
New York, NY 10011
USA

enslow.com

Published in 2020 by Enslow Publishing, LLC.
101 W. 23rd Street, Suite 240, New York, NY 10011

Library of Congress Cataloging-in-Publication Data

Names: Reilly, Kevin, author.
Title: Ports / Kevin Reilly.
Description: New York : Enslow Publishing, 2020. | Series: Exploring infrastructure | Audience: Grades 3-6. | Includes bibliographical references and index.
Identifiers: LCCN 2018020366| ISBN 9781978503373 (library bound) | ISBN 9781978505124 (pbk.)
Subjects: LCSH: Harbors—Juvenile literature. | CYAC: Harbors. | LCGFT: Instructional and educational works.
Classification: LCC HE551 .R45 2019 | DDC 387.1—dc23
LC record available at https://lccn.loc.gov/2018020366

Printed in the United States of America

To Our Readers: We have done our best to make sure all website addresses in this book were active and appropriate when we went to press. However, the author and the publisher have no control over and assume no liability for the material available on those websites or on any websites they may link to. Any comments or suggestions can be sent by email to customerservice@enslow.com.

Photo Credits: Cover, p. 1 tcly/Shutterstock.com; cover, pp. 1, 3 (top) Panimoni/Shutterstock.com; p. 5 Peter Hermes Furian/Shutterstock.com; p. 7 photoff/Shutterstock.com; p. 11 Universal Images Group/Getty Images; p. 12 Khufu Solar Boat (photo)/Bridgeman Images; p. 14 AFP/Getty Images; p. 18 Print Collector/Hulton Archive/Getty Images; p. 20 Bloomberg/Getty Images; p. 22 Bespaliy/Shutterstock.com; p. 26 Photocreo/Michal Bednarek/Shutterstock.com; p. 29 © iStockphoto.com/jtyler; p. 30 Patrick Foto/Shutterstock.com; p. 33 Liu Liqun/Corbis Documentary/Getty Images; p. 34 Visual China Group/Getty Images; p. 37 daa.riaa/Shutterstock.com; p. 39 Anton Petrus/Moment Open/Getty Images; p. 43 Joe Raedle/Getty Images.

CONTENTS

INTRODUCTION

A Journey into the Past

Imagine what the world was like a long, long time ago. There was no electricity or internet or television. People lived in small villages and towns near bodies of water. Most of them would live their whole lives without traveling more than a few miles from their homes.

When you live like that, the rest of the world might as well not exist! Your entire culture—your beliefs and customs—would come from the people who grew up in the exact same place that you did. That means that your food, traditions, and ideas would have nothing to do with anybody outside of your little town. Today, you can be an American who likes Greek food, Japanese video games, or Italian fashion. You have access to the whole world! You probably wouldn't enjoy living back when people's choices were so limited.

Thankfully, humans are good at coming up with new ideas, even when they are stuck in small groups. Since most early people lived

The Roman Empire
in 117 AD, at its greatest extent

Mare Germanicum

Britannia
Belgica
Germania Superior
Lugdunensis
nus
icus
Aquitania
Raetia
Noricum
Pannonia
Narbonensis
Dacia
Italia
Dalmatia
Moesia
Pontus Euxinus
Tarraconensis
Corsica
•Roma
Thracia
Macedonia
Armenia
tania
Sardinia
Epirus
Bithynia et Pontus
Baetica
Asia
Galatia
Cappadocia
Lycia
Cilicia
Sicilia
Achaia
Assyria
Africa
Mare Internum
Syria
Mauretania
Cyprus
Mesopotamia
Iudaea
Cyrenaica
Arabia Petraea
Aegyptus

The Mediterranean Sea during the Roman Empire. This area was full of ports for military and trading ships.

near water, they invented different types of boats to help them catch fish easier. It wasn't long before someone decided to use a boat to travel beyond their town. They would take a sturdy boat and fill it with lots of food and weapons. They would also bring along interesting inventions. If they met anyone, they would be able to make trades. They would convince their bravest friends to come with them and set sail on an adventure!

Let's pretend that we're on board the first boat that ever left our ancient town. We have no idea what we're going to find. Everything we know about the world is from the old stories that our elders like to tell us. We may have heard about a few people who left the town many years ago. They came back years later with strange foreign items and tales of their adventures.

There are other stories that we have been told. People made them up to explain strange happenings or to keep people from doing things that they thought were dangerous. Perhaps the towns-people didn't want children to be swimming too far out into the ocean, so they told them that horrifying sea monsters would eat them if they lost sight of the beach. We grew up hearing these stories and have no reason not to believe them.

But we're brave, so we press on anyway. After three days of sailing down the coast, another town appears in the distance. Its buildings look very different from ours, but in some ways similar. We can hear the noise as someone spots our boat. The whole town wants to see who we are. This makes us nervous. But we try to remember that our town would behave the same way if a strange boat appeared on the horizon.

Finally we make it to shore. The strongest men in the town surround our boat. They are holding weapons, but they look mainly curious. We try to speak with them, but our languages have nothing in common. It takes a little while, but soon we figure out how

A fishing boat in Greece. Soon after boats were invented, people began setting off to fish and, later, to explore.

to use hand movements and drawings to show that we don't mean them any harm. The strangers talk to each other, and they must decide that we aren't a threat. They bring us into the town. We eat a strange, delicious dinner with the wisest elders. We do our best to communicate with them.

After dinner, we show them the inventions and goods that we brought to trade. It turns out that they have a lot of the same types of weapons that we do, but they think our food is delicious! They are also amazed by the candles we brought along because they haven't invented them yet. Meanwhile, we notice that they have sturdy baskets made of some kind of reed that doesn't grow near our town. In the end, we trade them all of our candles for a huge bushel of dried reeds. Best of all, when we start to leave for home, one of the important men from their town climbs on board our ship. He wants to come with us!

Once we make it home, some of our people spend a lot of time with the foreign man. Soon, they have figured out how to speak with one another. The man tours our town. He notices that we have medicines that can help cure a sickness that has been affecting his townspeople. We give him medicine and a boat. In exchange, he promises to return with more reeds and some other inventions that we might find useful.

As the years go by, our two towns learn how to speak each other's languages. They even start to mix foreign words into their own slang! We start to rely on the inventions and resources we get when we trade with our new friends, and they start to rely on ours. After some time, we build big boats in order to ship goods from one town to the other. We build bigger docks so that the boats can stay in deeper water. We also make warehouses to store the materials we ship and receive. We have created a port!

As this story shows, ports were one of the most important structures in human civilization. They made people's lives much easier. They also improved the ways that people stepped outside of their own cultures and learned about other communities. Let's learn more.

Chapter 1

ANCIENT PORTS

The earliest humans were nomads. They never stayed in one place for very long. Instead, they would follow around herds of animals, which they would hunt for food. This took a lot of time and energy. People could not do much beyond finding food. Eventually, humans in fertile areas learned how to farm. This meant that they could stop following animals around and build permanent homes to live in. This happened in many different ways in different places around the world. But all of these early towns had at least one thing in common: they had to be close to water.

Water was needed for drinking and bathing. It was also very helpful in farming. Large bodies of water have lots of fish, which people learned how to catch and cook. As time went on, many communities learned how to build boats to help them fish. As we learned in the last chapter, once people invented boats, sooner or later they set out to explore areas around them. Since almost every early village or town was built near water, many people began to travel

An Egyptian wall painting shows sailors from ancient times.

farther afield. Traveling to other towns would often lead to alliances and trading, which led to the invention of ports.

A port is a facility built for loading and unloading ships. It is also the place where passengers are dropped off or picked up by ships. These places often have massive storage areas for the materials that are being shipped and received. They are usually built next to harbors. These are sheltered bodies of water where ships can be easily docked. These days, with our huge ships, we have to carefully pick a good harbor if we want to build a port. But in ancient times, boats were small. Almost anywhere the water was calm enough for people to build a town was a safe place to build a port, too.

Modern ports are usually connected to other transportation systems. These can be railroads, highways, or airports. This allows us to easily move goods all around the country—and the world. We'll learn much more about modern ports in later chapters, but the basic parts of ancient ports really weren't too different from the ones we have today.

The Oldest Port in the World

The oldest man-made port that we have discovered is Wadi al-Jarf in what is now Egypt. Wadi al-Jarf is located on the Red Sea. The water there is nice and calm. It's not far from where the Suez Canal was later built. (This was a very important shipping area that we'll discuss later.) Archaeologists think that Wadi al-Jarf is at least 4,500 years old!

We know that Wadi al-Jarf was a big port. How do we know this? More than one hundred anchors have been discovered in the water

This boat was built by the Egyptians and found thousands of years later in a pyramid. It is expertly made and strong enough to still sail today!

nearby. Archaeologists also found the ruins of several huge buildings that were most likely used as warehouses. They even found some fragments of ancient papyrus that tell us more about what life was like in the area at the time. These fragments are the oldest pieces of papyrus that have ever been found in Egypt.

Best of all, many jars have been found at Wadi al-Jarf. They were probably used to store goods on boats. The very same type of jar was discovered at a different archaeological site far across the sea. This gives us proof that the two towns were trading with one another!

Problems with Ancient Ports

More About Wadi al-Jarf

The ruins of Wadi al-Jarf were discovered by J. G. Wilkinson in 1832. Wilkinson was a British writer who was an expert on Egypt. At the time, he thought the ruins were Greek catacombs, an underground cemetery. He didn't look into them much further. Some amateur French archaeologists started to dig in the site in the 1950s, but they stopped their work because of a crisis in the region. It wasn't until their notes were published in 2008 that people became interested in the area again. Now we know that it was the oldest port in the world, and we've found the oldest Egyptian papyrus there, too. It was worth the wait!

Early ports were not nearly as efficient or well designed as the ones we have today. The main reason for this is that early people had

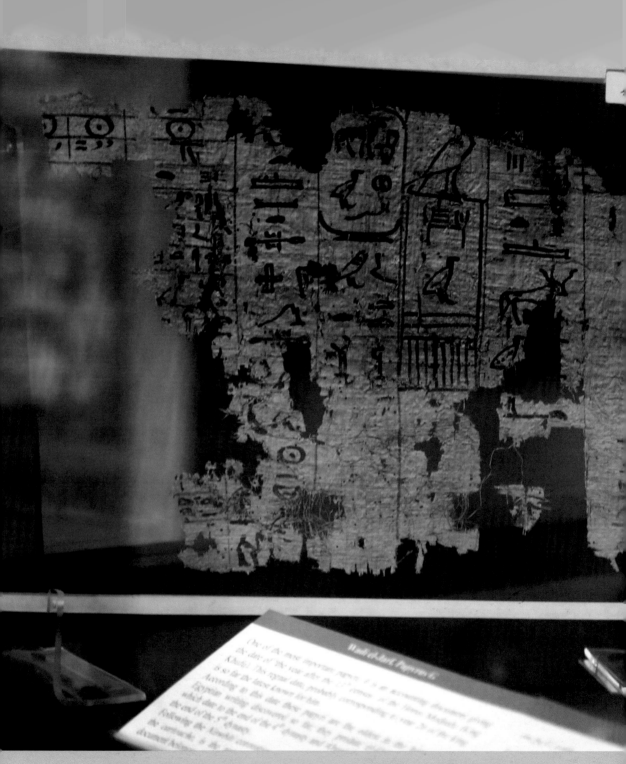

This papyrus (paper) was found at Wadi al-Jarf. Many of the Egyptian symbols on it are still clear enough to read.

limited technology. All of the work had to be done by hand, using very primitive tools. This mainly affected two major features of ports: ships and wharves.

Shipbuilding is an art that has taken thousands of years to perfect. Figuring out how to make a big structure float is very complicated. This is especially true when you want to load it up with as many goods as you can and make sure that it survives the journey to another town and back. On top of that, ancient people could only build ships with wood. The only building materials they could use were made from the trees that grew close to their towns. This meant that, depending on the type of wood, builders would be able to make small- to medium-sized boats that could hold a modest amount of cargo. To make up for this, they would have to send many more boats back and forth. This required lots of time, resources, and workers.

Wharves were the other element of ports that were much more basic in ancient times. A wharf is a structure on the shore of a harbor or on the bank of a river or canal where ships dock to load and unload cargo. Wharves are useful because they make it easier to dock a boat without ramming it into the land. But they also have another important purpose. The water is much deeper a little farther away from the shore than it is right next to it. Since the bottoms of larger boats sit much lower in the water than small ones, they need long wharves that stretch out into the middle of harbors.

This way, the ships can dock and unload large amounts of cargo. In the past, building a structure on top of the water was incredibly difficult, if not impossible. There was a limit to how far out builders could make wharves stretch. But the boats in ancient times were not very large, so the wharves did not have to be very long.

For many reasons, shipping in ancient times was a very slow, costly process that called for many workers. Thanks to modern technology, the ports of today have completely changed the business of shipping. In the next chapter, we'll take a closer look at the ways that people have improved ports over time.

Chapter 2

USING TECHNOLOGY TO IMPROVE PORTS

Modern ports have a lot in common with their ancient ancestors. They are still located in towns and cities that are built on harbors. They still have wharves where ships can dock and load and unload cargo. They still have large storage facilities for the goods that move through them. The main difference is size. Thanks to improved technology, everything about today's ports is much, much bigger.

From Jars to Storage Containers: Technology Transforms Ports

In the last chapter, we learned that the size of ports was limited in ancient times. Everything needed to be built by hand using nearby

This print shows the Port of Shanghai in 1847. It went on to become one of the busiest ports in the world.

materials. We also discussed how it would have been hard for our ancestors to build very long wharves. Today, we are not limited to using the trees that grow nearby to build our structures. We can use all kinds of different materials from all over the world! We have also invented special types of plastic that can float even when they are supporting a lot of weight. This technology means that we can build wharves that stretch hundreds of feet out into harbors, where the water is much deeper.

Today, we can use wharves to transport goods from ships that are far away from shore. This means that we can also build and use much larger ships than ancient civilizations could have imagined. Today's cargo ships are like huge floating cities. They can move thousands of tons of cargo with ease. They carry enough fuel to travel across oceans without stopping. Modern ships are also made of very durable metals, instead of wood, so they are much sturdier. They also don't need to be repaired as often.

There is one more feature of ports that has been transformed by technology. That is the container that holds the cargo. At Wadi al-Jarf, clay jars were used to move goods from one port to another. As the centuries passed, we began to build chests and crates for this purpose. Today, we have greatly improved how goods are transported and stored. This was done with one amazing

The Largest Cargo Ship of the Modern Age

The *OOCL Hong Kong* is the world's largest cargo ship. It was built in 2017. The ship is over 1,300 feet (396 meters) long, 190 feet (58 m) wide, and 106 feet (32 m) tall. Fifty-two feet (16 m) of its height is below water at all times. At full capacity, the *OOCL Hong Kong* can hold an incredible 21,413 shipping containers! Ancient sailors would never believe it, but this giant ship only needs a crew of eighteen people to operate.

The *OOCL Hong Kong* is the largest cargo ship in the world. Each one of those rectangular containers is the size of a truck!

invention: the intermodal container. It is commonly known as the shipping container.

A shipping container is a large rectangular storage unit. It is usually made from steel. It is built and designed for intermodal freight transport. The word "intermodal" means that the container can be moved several different ways—by ship, train, and truck. This makes it very easy to move cargo all around the world. Shipping containers come in a few standard sizes. These sizes are the same around the world so that countries can design their vehicles to carry the same types of containers. Best of all, these containers are able to stack together. This makes them ideal for both transportation and storage. There are more than twenty million shipping containers worldwide. They store more than 60 percent of all goods that are shipped by sea today.

New Innovations

As you can see, engineers, scientists, and inventors have improved just about every part of ports since ancient times. But there are also many features of ports that were created much more recently.

In the past, goods were mostly traded between towns and cities with ports. But there were also many people who lived in the countryside around the port. They would have to travel into town to buy things that came from abroad. These days, people everywhere buy things that come from all around the world! This shift in the way that trade works could have made ports useless. Instead, ports adapted to the new system. Unlike their ancestors, modern ports need more than just a harbor to be successful. They are located near highways, railroads, and airports. Goods can arrive by sea, move through the facility, and be transferred to another type of transportation. A truck, train, or airplane can then transport the goods closer to their destination. That's why having a standard shipping container that can be used in many different ways is so important! It takes a lot of planning and resources to make these huge transportation systems work. We'll learn a lot more in the next

Container cranes stand ready to unload cargo from a ship.

chapter about the skilled workers who make sure that everything runs smoothly.

There are also several machines that have become necessary to ports in the modern age. In the past, anything that arrived at a port would have to be carried off of the ship by hand. This was back-breaking work. Many strong workers were needed just to handle a single shipment. Today, we have many types of utility vehicles that do the hard work for us. Ports have fleets of large forklifts to help move things from one place to another. They also have tugboats that make it easier to dock huge cargo ships at their wharves. These inventions make ports much safer and more efficient than they ever were before.

Perhaps the most important machine at any modern port is the container crane. A container crane is a gigantic crane that is built on the edge of a port's dock. Its job is to move shipping containers. These huge cranes can move all along a wharf to pick up containers wherever they are located. They have special tools called spreaders. The spreader locks into the tops of shipping containers. The crane can then lift the containers high into the air and move them without fear of them falling and causing an accident. Ports have had basic cranes since the Middle Ages. But they cannot begin to compare to the cranes that are used at today's ports.

You've learned all about the new technology that is present in modern ports. Now let's focus on the most important part of any type of infrastructure: the workers who build them and keep them running efficiently!

Chapter 3

WHO WORKS AT PORTS?

In the last chapter, we learned all about how ports have changed over the years. They have become more advanced and efficient since the earliest ones were built. These improvements are great for society. But they also make building, operating, and maintaining ports a lot more complicated. Let's take a look at some careers that involve making sure that modern ports are safe, productive, and well built.

Construction and Maintenance

In the past, ports were built by general laborers and sailors. Remember that the earliest warehouses, wharves, and ships were much simpler than they are today. This meant that experienced builders could construct and repair ports without having lots of special training.

Today, building and maintaining the different parts of ports is much more difficult. Some general construction workers are still needed. But port engineers are in charge of most of these projects. These engineers specialize in the planning, design, construction, and repair of ports. This includes the structures, machines, and ships. They are also responsible for making sure that the right permits are issued for each project. They regularly inspect everything to make sure that it is safe. As you know, ports involve structures on land as well as different types of ships. Port engineers need to have a lot of knowledge, education, and talent to do their jobs well.

Basic Operations

Early ports needed hundreds of workers to run well. All of the cargo that needed to be moved to and from ships was carried by hand a little bit at a time. This work was difficult, sometimes dangerous, and it took a lot of time. But any person who was willing and able could do it. Ships were much smaller then, but they needed a crew of dozens of sailors to travel. Again, everything was done by hand, including rowing the boat! Shipwrecks were also much more common because ships were built with weaker materials.

Modern ports still use general laborers and sailors. But thanks to new technology, not as many workers are needed to run the daily operations. This is quite impressive because the ports of today handle a lot more goods than ancient port workers could have

A port engineer oversees the maintenance, inspection, and repair of ships. He or she also makes sure that all safety rules are followed at the port.

imagined. They also do it much more safely. Today's sailors and port workers have much more training than workers did in the past. Training is very important because workers have to operate complicated machinery and keep track of many shipments.

Oversight

In the last chapter, we learned about how complicated modern ports have become. Many large ships load and unload cargo every day. The cargo must then be stored. On top of that, ports act as transportation hubs that connect land, sea, and air. (A hub is a center of activity.) Ports must work with shipyards, railroads, truck fleets, and airports. These are also very complicated systems. They all need to be running smoothly in order for ports to run well.

Who's in charge of all of these systems? The United States and other countries knew that ports were very important and complex. They did not want separate private companies to control trucking, railroads, and other systems. They thought that it would make communication and teamwork between the groups harder. They believed that the ports would not run well that way. So they created organizations called port authorities. These groups are owned by the states. They control everything connected with the ports they oversee.

The port authority has a lot of responsibility. It receives, stores, ships, and protects all of the goods and passengers that travel through its transportation hub. This involves many different types of workers, depending on which part of the port they are overseeing. All of the workers must be well trained and organized. They also need to be able to work well as a team. Everyone has to be on the same page so that the port can run as smoothly as possible.

The Harbormaster

One port worker who has a big job is the harbormaster. Harbormasters are in charge of making sure that all of the rules are followed within a harbor. It is very important that everyone on the water behaves safely and properly. The harbormaster make sure ships and passengers are safe and the harbor is secure. He or she will also help respond in case of emergencies. Harbormasters are expert sailors with lots of experience, either in the military or merchant navy. They answer only to the Coast Guard.

Security

Let's look at one more job that is necessary to keep ports running smoothly. It is one that was much less important in ancient times: security. Many items come into the country at ports. Customs workers are in charge of making sure that nothing dangerous or illegal makes it past their team. In the past, borders between countries were much less defined. Also, not as many things were illegal. This means that customs wasn't a big issue for the ports of ancient times.

A harbormaster has many responsibilities. These include ensuring safety and security in the port and on ships, as well as keeping ship traffic moving smoothly.

A worker oversees a shipment of containers that has arrived at the port.

Port security teams are always on the lookout for any kind of danger. Ports are very important to the way that we live our lives. If an enemy destroyed them, they could cripple an entire area within days. Thankfully, security workers have modern technology, trained dogs, and a lot of experience. These allow them to keep a close eye out for any suspicious activities at all times.

We've learned about the different jobs that are a big part of keeping ports efficient and safe. Now let's take a look at some of the most impressive ports in the world today!

Chapter 4

THE GREATEST PORTS ON EARTH

People have been building and rebuilding ports all around the world for five thousand years. Remember the simple docks we talked about in the first chapter? Today, they are centers of activity for transportation and shipping. They are able to quickly handle an incredible amount of goods. Then they send them halfway around the world! Let's learn about the most remarkable and fascinating ports in the modern world.

Busiest Ports

One of the greatest ports on earth is the Port of Shanghai in China. It is the busiest container port in the world. It won that title in 2010 when it handled over twenty-nine million shipping containers in a single year. That is half a million more than the Port of Singapore, the previous titleholder. But it doesn't end there. In 2016, the Port

The Port of Shanghai handles more shipping
containers than any other port in the world.

of Shanghai beat its own record by handling more than thirty-seven
million shipping containers! That's about 514 million tons (466.2 million metric tons) of cargo that was shipped and received in the port.

The Port of Shanghai became the busiest port for several reasons. Its ability to handle tons of cargo shows that it is very efficient. But another major factor is location. Shanghai is on the East
China Sea, and three major rivers also come together nearby. This
means there is a lot of traffic coming through. Shanghai has been

The Port of Ningbo-Zhoushan handles more cargo
than any other port in terms of weight.

a port city for a couple thousand years. It has had a lot of time to perfect its operations.

American ports aren't as huge as the biggest ones in China. But they still manage to process large amounts of cargo. The busiest cargo port in the United States is the Port of South Louisiana. It is located between Baton Rogue and New Orleans on the Mississippi River. This port is the third greatest in the world by total trade. This makes it a huge boost to the American economy. It's especially important for the Midwest because 60 percent of the grain that its farms export goes through the Port of South Louisiana.

The United States does have one of the busiest ports in the world, when you look at it another way. PortMiami is located in Miami, Florida. It is the busiest cruise port in the world and the busiest passenger port. Over four million passengers travel through the port every year, mostly on massive cruise ships. PortMiami employs almost 176,000 workers and contributes $17 billion to the local economy each year.

Unique Ports

Handling tons of cargo or passengers is not the only way a port can stand out. Some remarkable ports are very old, some are very new, and some are just located in very strange places.

The McMurdo Station harbor definitely fits in the last category. McMurdo Station is on an island in Antarctica. It is the largest

Port of Ningbo-Zhoushan

You have learned that the Port of Shanghai moves the most shipping containers every year. But there is another Chinese port that is quite busy as well. The Port of Ningbo-Zhoushan is also located on the East China Sea. It sits between several major canals and shipping routes. A lot of manufacturing materials go through this port. It handles more cargo in terms of weight than any other port in the world; 889 million tons (806.4 million metric tons) of cargo go through the port every year!

community on the continent, with over one hundred buildings, a science station, and both of the ATMs in Antarctica. Scientists and researchers come from around the world to study the area's unique ecosystem. But it is not easy to live in a remote place like this. In fact, it is only possible because of the station's active harbor. It keeps the scientists and explorers well stocked with supplies and prepared for anything!

The final unique port we'll take a look at is Byblos Port in Lebanon. It is not a large port by today's standards. But the Lebanese people believe that it was originally built in 3000 BCE. That makes it over five thousand years old! It is the oldest port in the world that is still operating. Byblos Port was also quite important in ancient times. Most of the wood used for construction in the Eastern Mediterranean Sea was shipped through there, helping many towns build up their infrastructure. Even cooler, wood shipped through

The harbor at McMurdo Station in Antarctica is very important to the people who work there. Ships come in to the remote port bringing much-needed supplies.

Byblos Port was used to build the tombs of ancient Egyptian pharaohs!

By now, we've learned a lot about why ports are so important. In the final chapter, we'll take some time to think about what our world would be like without them.

Chapter 5

A WORLD WITHOUT PORTS

In the introduction, we imagined what the world must have been like before ports were invented. We saw how mixing with other cultures and getting new materials and inventions benefitted our ancient town. But you may have wondered if things were really so bad before we set sail on our adventures. Our ancestors knew how to farm, and we had a town with everything we needed. Wouldn't life have been fine if we'd never met up with people of other cultures?

Before ports were invented, ancient people were able to survive without them. If ports disappeared today, it would be a very different story. This book has taken a look at all of the good that ports do for people around the world. But the best way to understand how important ports are is to imagine a world without them.

An abandoned pier in a Russian village. Ports are important lifelines for communities. Without them, the entire area suffers.

Scenario One: New York City

Let's say we live in the middle of Manhattan in New York City. We love it here because everything is so convenient. You can find just about anything you want from all around the world if you look hard enough. If ports disappeared tomorrow, things would be very different.

We All Rely on Ports

Is there any place in America that does not rely on ports? If you live in a farming community with some factories nearby, maybe not having ports would not affect you right away. But soon, you would realize that almost everything you own traveled through a port at some point. Even those factories and farms have to use supplies and materials that came from somewhere else. No matter what, without ports our lives would get much more difficult.

There aren't any large farms in New York City. There aren't many factories that still operate there, either. Almost everything that is bought or sold in New York comes from somewhere else first. How does it get there? It passes through the port system. Without ports, the city would run out of almost everything very quickly. The almost nine million people who live there would have a big problem.

Too many people and not enough resources is a very bad combination. Suppose we wake up and the morning news tells us that ports don't exist anymore. What's the first thing we would do? Most people would probably go to the grocery store to stock up on food. But most people would probably have the same idea. Food would run out very quickly. Soon, there would be a huge crowd of angry, desperate people. Things could become dangerous.

Even if we imagine that food wouldn't run out, other disasters could happen if there were no ports. Let's think about no medicine. Almost no medicine of any kind is made in New York City. There isn't space for those kinds of facilities, so medicine is brought in from other places. Without ports, the supply of medicine would slowly dwindle down to nothing. Many people would find themselves in a crisis.

Food, medicine, building supplies, clothing—we need all of these things in order to live. And there's not enough made in New York City to provide for nine million people. In time, the only choice would be to leave. But the roads would be jammed with cars, and the local port authority is in charge of lots of the public transportation that leaves the city. It's also in charge of the bridges, tunnels, and airports! We would have no choice but to walk somewhere that ports aren't critical for our survival.

Scenario Two: Puerto Rico

New York City may seem like the worst place in America that you could be if ports disappeared tomorrow. It definitely wouldn't be ideal. But New York has an advantage over some other places: at least in New York, you could try to leave.

This time, let's imagine that we wake up to the bad news in San Juan, Puerto Rico. San Juan is a very important port. Ports are very important to Puerto Rico. In fact, *Puerto Rico* means "Rich Port" in Spanish. When you live on an island, many of your basic needs are brought in from other places. This is especially true when your island is a major port.

If ports no longer existed in Puerto Rico, resources would become very hard to find almost overnight. People would fight over the few boats left on the island. (Remember, any boat that is connected to a port no longer exists.) Before long, millions of people would be stranded. We would have to hunt for food and materials that are found naturally in Puerto Rico. But as time passed, animals would become extinct and every piece of fruit on the island would be gone. It wouldn't take long for the vibrant community of Puerto Rico to become a desert island.

Things would get even worse if a disaster occurred. Puerto Rico is still recovering from the damage caused by Hurricane Maria in 2017. In that case, the island was able to bring in huge ships filled with supplies. Volunteers traveled to the island to help out. Without ports, large ships would not be able to dock within swimming distance of the island. We would be in a dangerous situation if ports no longer existed in Puerto Rico.

After Hurricane Maria in 2017, the ports of Puerto Rico were used to bring in large ships containing supplies, medicine, and workers.

Thankfully, ports are a major part of our world's infrastructure. Even better, they'll still be here when we wake up tomorrow. The fact that we couldn't continue to live our lives without them is proof of how amazing and important ports are. Hopefully, the information you learned in this book will help you to appreciate what a large role ports play in every person's life.

CHRONOLOGY

3000 BCE Byblos Port is built in Lebanon. It is the oldest port still operating today.

2570 BCE Wadi al-Jarf is built in Egypt.

600 BCE Piraeus becomes the home of the Athenian fleet and the most important port in ancient Greece.

1838 William Armstrong invents the first hydraulic crane. It will be used to move large shipping containers.

1896 The Board of Commissioners of the Port of New Orleans, the port authority in the region, is chartered.

1902 Development begins on the Port of Miami in Miami, Florida.

1948 The US Army Transportation Corps develops an early version of the modern standardized shipping container.

2016 The Port of Shanghai processes over thirty-seven million shipping containers, breaking its own record as the busiest port in the world.

GLOSSARY

container crane A gigantic crane built on the edge of a port's dock that is specifically designed to move shipping containers.

culture The beliefs and customs of a group or society.

harbor Sheltered body of water where ships can be easily docked.

harbormaster The official that is in charge of enforcing all of the rules within a harbor.

port A facility built for loading and unloading ships, as well as for dropping off and picking up passengers.

port authority A state-run agency that is in charge of overseeing all operations of a port.

port engineer Engineer that specializes in the planning, design, construction, and repair of the structures, machines, and vessels that are used in a port.

shipping container A large rectangular storage unit, usually made from steel, that is built and designed for intermodal freight transport.

warehouse A large building designed for organizing and storing goods.

wharf A structure on the shore of a harbor or on the bank of a river or canal where ships dock to load and unload cargo.

FURTHER READING

Books

Flammang, James M. *Cargo Ships.* Ann Arbor, MI: Cherry Lake, 2008.

Gitlin, Marty. *Infrastructure of America's Ports, Harbors, and Dams.* New York, NY: Mitchell Lane, 2018.

Kent, Deborah. *U.S. Infrastructure.* New York, NY: Children's Press, 2013.

Yomtov, Nel. *Transportation Planner.* Ann Arbor, MI: Cherry Lake, 2013.

Websites

Harbor and Port

kids.britannica.com/students/article/harbor-and-port/274773

Explains types of ports and harbors, examines daily operations, and describes world's greatest ports.

National Geographic Encyclopedia: Harbors

www.nationalgeographic.org/encyclopedia/harbor

A comprehensive overview of ports and harbors

Ports and Harbors

www.waterencyclopedia.com/Po-Re/Ports-and-Harbors.html

Focuses on American ports and harbors.

INDEX